MUSHROOMS

MUSHROOMS

INTRODUCTION BY SUE LAWRENCE

southwater

This edition is published by Southwater

Southwater is an imprint of
Anness Publishing Limited
Hermes House
88–89 Blackfriars Road
London SE1 8HA
tel. 020 7401 2077
fax 020 7633 9499

Distributed in the UK by
The Manning Partnership
251–253 London Road East
Batheaston
Bath BA1 7RL
tel. 01225 852 727
fax 01225 852 852

Distributed in the USA by
Anness Publishing Inc.
27 West 20th Street
Suite 504
New York
NY 10011
tel. 212 807 6739
fax 212 807 6813

Distributed in Australia by
Sandstone Publishing
Unit 1
360 Norton Street
Leichhardt
New South Wales 2040
tel. 02 9560 7888
fax 02 9560 7488

1 3 5 7 9 10 8 6 4 2

Publisher Joanna Lorenz
Senior Cookery Editor Linda Fraser
Cookery Editor Anne Hildyard
Designer Lisa Tai
Illustrations Anna Koska

Photographers Karl Adamson, David Armstrong, Steve Baxter, James Duncan, Michelle Garrett, Nelson Hargreaves and Amanda Heywood
Recipes Alex Barker, Carla Capalbo, Elizabeth Wolf-Cohen, Shirley Gill, Norma MacMillan, Liz Trigg, Laura Washburn, Steven Wheeler and Pamela Westland
Food for photography Elizabeth Wolf-Cohen, Carole Handslip, Wendy Lee and Jane Stevenson
Stylists Madeleine Brehaut, Blake Minton and Kirsty Rawlings

For all recipes, quantities are given in both metric and imperial measures and, where appropriate, measures are also given in standard cups and spoons. Follow one set, but not a mixture, because they are not interchangeable.

Previously published as *Cooking With Mushrooms*

Contents

Introduction

They like to be kept in the dark. All fungi do. Most of the mushrooms we eat are cultivated ones which are grown in controlled darkness, to keep their pure white colour. Wild mushrooms usually grow in dark or shaded woodlands. Until some years ago, we too were kept in the dark about all the different varieties on offer. It was button mushrooms or nothing for most of us. But now there is a cornucopia of wild and cultivated mushrooms out there, all ready for the picking.

I have vivid memories of mushroom picking in the woods of north Finland. Here the Finns come out every autumn to pick both mushrooms and berries, to sustain them through the hard winter ahead. The mushrooms are either dried or salted and used in all sorts of savoury dishes; from reindeer stews to creamy mushroom pie. Elsewhere in Europe, keen mycologists have trundled out in the autumn to pick the fine offerings of nearby woods. But in Britain, it is only recently that we have become aware of the marvellous potential out there. Now we can not only choose from an extensive array of cultivated mushrooms, but also from the many varieties of fresh and dried wild ones, many of which are picked in this country. We too are getting the mushroom-picking bug.

There are now cultivated chestnut, oyster and shiitake mushrooms to add to the button mushrooms. Wild ones, such as ceps or morels are often to be seen for sale in good delicatessens or greengrocers and also on restaurant menus all over the country. Instead of having mushrooms as merely garnish, they are given pride of place. The meaty texture of many types means they make excellent additions to stews, casseroles or sauces. Their affinity with both butter and olive oil means they are also often cooked very simply and served alone, perhaps with a sprinkling of fresh parsley.

In this book, you will also find more innovative dishes: Muffins with Sole and Mushrooms, Tuna Shiitake Teriyaki, Pasta with Mushrooms and Chorizo, for example. But there are also interesting interpretations of the classics, such as Mushroom and Bacon Risotto, Macaroni Cheese with Mushrooms, and Spinach and Mushroom Roulade. There are good combinations with fresh herbs – Salmon with Tarragon and Mushrooms, and Crunchy Mushrooms with Dill Dip.

It would be difficult to find more versatile vegetables than mushrooms; they please carnivores and vegetarians alike. Their role varies: it can both enhance and dominate. The humble mushroom might live its life in the dark, but it certainly brings sunshine to the plate.

Sue Lawrence

*T*YPES OF *M*USHROOM

SLICED BUTTON MUSHROOMS

The flavour is very mild, and they are good sliced and eaten raw in salads.

CLOSED CUP MUSHROOMS

Good eaten raw or lightly cooked in stir-fries.

OPEN CUP MUSHROOMS

At this stage the brown gills are showing and the cap is darker. Good for stuffing and baking.

FLAT MUSHROOMS

When the cap is quite flat, mushrooms have the best flavour. This makes them ideal for soup.

CANNED BUTTON MUSHROOMS

These make a useful addition to soups, stews, pasta and rice dishes.

SHIITAKE MUSHROOMS

These are of Asian origin and are moist and fleshy with a strong flavour.

OYSTER MUSHROOMS

Moist, delicate pale grey or yellow flesh, they are so named because they are thought to resemble oyster shells.

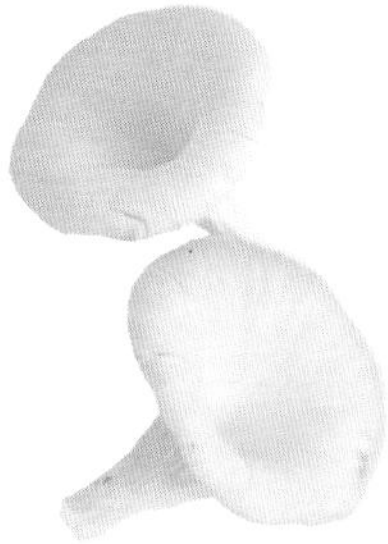

MORELS

These are intensely perfumed, expensive and beloved of gourmets. They are hard to come by but only a few are needed. Morels are available dried.

BOLETUS, CEP OR PORCINI

The boletus has a round brown cap and thick stem. It is strongly flavoured, and is often dried.

CHESTNUT MUSHROOMS

All-purpose mushrooms with brown caps, also known as *champignons de Paris*.

PRESERVED MUSHROOMS

Wild varieties are often preserved in oil and sometimes roasted over charcoal first. Good for antipasto.

Preserved mushrooms
Sliced button mushrooms
Chestnut mushrooms
Open cup mushrooms
Yellow oyster mushrooms
Button mushrooms
Shiitake mushrooms
Closed cup mushrooms
Dried ceps
Canned button mushrooms
Dried morels
Grey oyster mushrooms
Flat mushrooms
Preserved mushrooms
Chestnut mushrooms

Basic Techniques

PREPARING MUSHROOMS

Both cultivated and wild mushrooms will have some soil or sand clinging to them. They absorb water easily and must not be allowed to become waterlogged, however those with deep gills or pockets, such as morels, can be soaked for a few minutes to remove any grit.

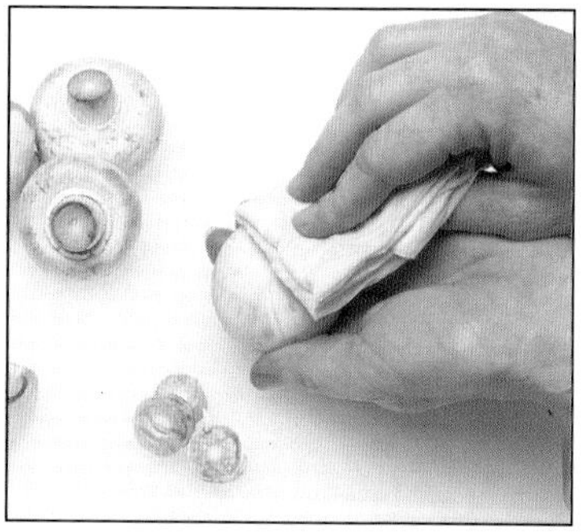

Trim the stem ends from wild mushrooms only if they are bruised. Small mushrooms can be left whole; larger ones can be sliced or chopped.

Rinse or wipe mushrooms with a damp cloth or kitchen paper.

DRYING MUSHROOMS

Drying mushrooms is a method of preservation that causes the essential flavours and aromas to intensify. The dried mushrooms will keep in an airtight jar for many months and can be added to soups and stews.

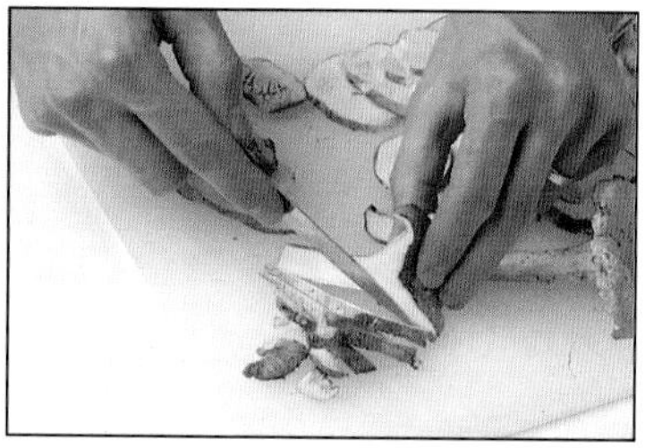

Wipe the mushrooms with a damp cloth or kitchen paper and cut away any parts that are damaged or bruised. Using a sharp knife, slice the mushrooms thinly.

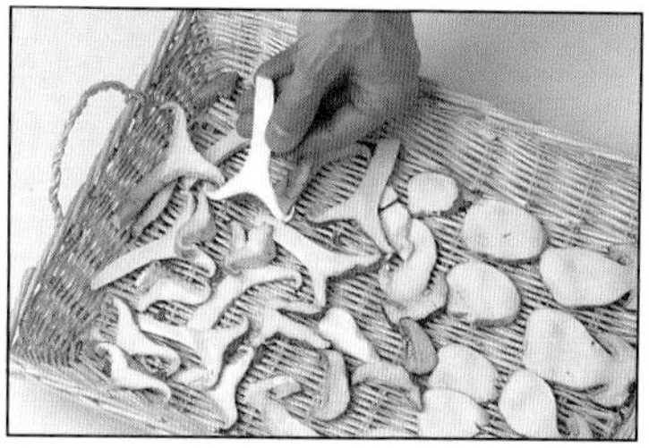

Arrange the sliced mushrooms in a single layer on a basket tray or baking sheet lined with newspaper and non-stick baking paper. Put the tray in a warm, airy place for two days.

Place the dried mushrooms in an air-tight, clean jar, label and store in a dark place. If the mushrooms are not completely dry, moulds may develop in storage. Check them before using.

COOKING MUSHROOMS

Nutritionally, mushrooms contain very little but protein. They are valued for their strong, distinctive flavour and particular chewy texture when cooked. Only the common mushroom can be eaten raw with safety. Cultivated or shop-bought wild mushrooms should always be cooked. Because they produce a lot of liquid and shrink in size, mushrooms are best cooked by first lightly sautéeing them in butter or olive oil, which seals in their flavour.

FREEZING MUSHROOMS

Mushrooms can be frozen successfully as they retain their flavour when thawed. Firmer varieties such as shiitake, closed cup and flat mushrooms are suitable candidates for freezing. Thaw them by dropping them briefly into boiling water just before use.

Ensure mushrooms are clean and free from grit and insects. Slice them thickly if they are large. Drop them into a pan of boiling salted water for 1 minute. Remove and drain well. Open freeze on a tray for 30–40 minutes. Store them in plastic bags or rigid containers in the freezer for up to six months.

Cook's Tips

- *Buying fresh*: Choose mushrooms that are firm and moist but without damp patches or dry stalk ends. Some wild mushroom varieties may have worms; these are not harmful and can be cut away before cooking. To establish if any are present, break off the stems of a few and cut through the caps.

- *Storing fresh*: Mushrooms do not store well if they become wet or sweaty. Store them in a refrigerator in a paper bag or covered with a damp cloth. They keep for up to four days in this way. Clean mushrooms before using in recipes.

- *Dried mushrooms*: These keep indefinitely in an airtight container in a cool place. Before use, soak them in tepid water for 25–30 minutes or add them directly to soups.

PICKLED MUSHROOMS

Pickling mushrooms preserves them as immersing them in vinegar inhibits any bacterial growth. This recipe gives the mushrooms a Chinese flavour, and firm varieties such as shiitake or chestnut mushrooms can be used.

Bring 250ml/8fl oz/1 cup white wine vinegar and 150ml/¼ pint/⅔ cup water to the boil in a stainless steel pan. Add 5ml/1 tsp salt, 1 chopped red chilli, 10ml/2 tsp coriander seeds, and 250g/9oz firm mushrooms (halved if large) and simmer for ten minutes. Cool.

Sterilize a small preserving jar with boiling water. Drain until dry. Place the mushrooms and their liquid in the jar, seal, label and leave for at least ten days to mature.

MAKING A MUSHROOM GARNISH

Mushrooms make an attractive garnish when they are fluted. To do this you will need to use very fresh white mushrooms and a small, sharp knife. The fluted mushrooms are then rubbed with lemon juice to prevent them from turning brown, or cooked *à blanc* (see right), or they can be sautéed in butter.

Using a small, sharp knife, and holding the blade at an angle, cut away a thin strip from the centre to the edge of the cap. Continue in this way evenly around the mushroom, removing the parings. Trim the stem flat.

PRESERVING MUSHROOMS IN OIL

Preserving mushrooms in oil may seem an extravagance, but the following recipe makes a delicious condiment. The oil is so full of flavour it can be used to make salad dressings. It will keep for up to 1 year.

Bring 250ml/8fl oz/1 cup white wine vinegar and 150ml/$\frac{1}{4}$ pint/$\frac{2}{3}$ cup water to the boil in a stainless steel pan. Add 5ml/1 tsp salt, 1 thyme sprig and 1 bay leaf. Infuse for 15 minutes. Add 450g/1lb assorted mushrooms and simmer for ten minutes.

Lift the mushrooms out of the liquid, drain well and place in a small, sterilized preserving jar.

Cover the mushrooms with 400ml/14fl oz/1$\frac{2}{3}$ cups olive oil, cover and label.

Mushroom Tips

- Keep mushrooms white by cooking *à blanc* with lemon juice, salt and pepper and a little water.
- Use the soaking liquid from dried mushrooms to add flavour to sauces and stocks.
- Add dried mushrooms to fresh for extra flavour.
- Add a few mushrooms to stuffings, soups and stir-fries. Serve cooked mushrooms as a vegetable with meat, fish, poultry or game dishes.
- Always buy wild mushrooms from an authenticated source, and never pick and eat wild mushrooms unless they have been identified by an expert.

Starters and Snacks

Mushrooms add scented flavour to delicious snacks; just simply served on toast, in a creamy soup, with a crisp crunchy coating, stuffed with garlic butter, or with sole as a splendid starter.

MUSHROOMS ON TOAST

Mushrooms have a happy relationship with garlic, but too often the intense flavour of the garlic takes over. The garlic here is tempered with a generous amount of fresh parsley and a touch of lemon.

Serves 4

30ml/2 tbsp unsalted butter, plus extra for spreading
1 onion, chopped
1 garlic clove, crushed
350g/12oz assorted mushrooms, such as button, chestnut and shiitake, trimmed and sliced
45ml/3 tbsp dry sherry
75ml/5 tbsp chopped fresh parsley
15ml/1 tbsp lemon juice
4 slices brown or white bread
salt and ground black pepper

Melt the butter in a large non-stick frying pan, add the onion and fry over a low heat without letting it colour.

Add the garlic and mushrooms, cover and cook for 3–5 minutes. Add the sherry and cook uncovered to evaporate the liquid.

Stir in the chopped fresh parsley and lemon juice, and then season to taste with salt and pepper.

Toast the bread and spread generously with butter. Serve immediately with the mushrooms spooned over the toast.

COOK'S TIP

Flat leaf parsley has a good flavour and keeps well in the fridge. To keep it really fresh, stand it in a jar of water and cover with a plastic bag.

CRUNCHY MUSHROOMS WITH DILL DIP

These crisp bites are ideal as an informal starter or served with drinks.

Serves 4–6

115g/4oz/2 cups fresh fine white breadcrumbs
25ml/1½ tbsp finely grated mature Cheddar cheese
5ml/1 tsp paprika
225g/8oz button mushrooms
2 egg whites

For the tomato and dill dip

4 ripe tomatoes
115g/4oz/½ cup curd cheese
60ml/4 tbsp natural low-fat yogurt
1 garlic clove, crushed
30ml/2 tbsp chopped fresh dill
salt and ground black pepper
dill sprig, to garnish

Preheat the oven to 190°C/375°F/Gas 5. Mix the breadcrumbs, cheese and paprika together in a bowl.

Wipe the mushrooms clean and trim the stalks, if necessary. Lightly whisk the egg whites with a fork, until frothy.

Dip each mushroom into the egg whites, then into the breadcrumb mixture. Repeat until all the mushrooms are coated.

Place the mushrooms on a non-stick baking sheet. Bake in the preheated oven for 15 minutes, or until tender and the coating has turned golden and crunchy.

To make the dip, score the bases of the tomatoes with a sharp knife. Plunge them into a saucepan of boiling water for 1 minute, then into a saucepan of cold water. Remove the skins. Halve the tomatoes, remove the seeds and cores and roughly chop the flesh.

Put the curd cheese, yogurt, garlic clove and dill into a mixing bowl and stir to combine thoroughly. Season to taste with salt and black pepper. Add the chopped tomatoes and stir to combine. Spoon the mixture into a serving dish and garnish with a sprig of fresh dill. Serve the mushrooms hot, together with the dip.

STUFFED MUSHROOMS

These mushrooms are perfect for dinner parties, or serve them in larger portions as a light supper dish.

Serves 4

350g/12oz large button mushrooms, stems removed
3 garlic cloves, crushed
175g/6oz/¾ cup butter, softened
50g/2oz/1 cup fresh white breadcrumbs
50g/2oz/1 cup chopped fresh parsley
1 egg, beaten
salt and cayenne pepper
8 cherry tomatoes, to garnish

Preheat the oven to 190°C/375°F/Gas 5. Arrange the mushrooms cup-side uppermost on a baking sheet. Mix the garlic and butter in a small bowl and divide 115g/4oz/½ cup of the garlic butter among the mushrooms.

Melt the remaining butter in a large, non-stick frying pan, add the breadcrumbs and lightly fry until golden brown. Place the chopped parsley in a bowl, add the breadcrumbs, season to taste with salt and pepper and mix together well.

Stir in the egg and use the mixture to fill the mushroom caps. Bake for 10–15 minutes until the topping has browned and the mushrooms have softened. Serve garnished with the tomatoes cut into quarters.

COOK'S TIP

If you are planning ahead, stuffed mushrooms can be prepared up to 12 hours in advance and kept in the fridge before baking.

Mushroom Soup

The chestnut mushrooms give additional flavour to this delicious, mixed mushroom soup.

Serves 4

60ml/4 tbsp unsalted butter
4 shallots or 1 onion, chopped
225g/8oz oyster and button mushrooms, trimmed and chopped
1 garlic clove, crushed
900ml/1½ pints/3¾ cups chicken stock, boiling
175g/6oz chestnut mushrooms, trimmed and sliced
60ml/4 tbsp double cream
30ml/2 tbsp lemon juice
salt and ground black pepper
45ml/3 tbsp chopped fresh parsley, to garnish
crusty bread, to serve

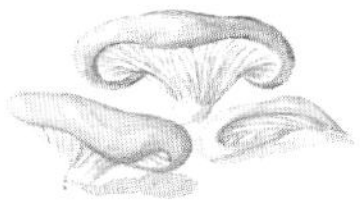

Melt half of the butter in a saucepan, add the shallots or onion and cook gently without letting them colour. Add the oyster and button mushrooms and garlic, and fry until soft and the juices begin to run. Add the chicken stock, bring back to the boil and simmer for 15 minutes. Place in a food processor or blender, and process until smooth. Return to the saucepan.

Melt the remaining butter in a non-stick frying pan, add the chestnut mushrooms and gently fry over a low heat without letting them colour. Add to the saucepan and simmer for a further minute.

Stir in the cream, sharpen with lemon juice, then season to taste with salt and pepper. Serve, ladled into four warmed soup bowls, sprinkled with parsley and accompanied by crusty bread.

MUFFINS WITH SOLE AND MUSHROOMS

Muffins, frozen spinach and a few mushrooms form the base for this satisfying snack. Any flat fish will do, although sole works best of all.

Serves 2

115g/4oz/½ cup butter, plus extra for buttering muffins
1 onion, chopped
115g/4oz brown button mushrooms, sliced
2 fresh thyme sprigs, chopped
275g/10oz frozen leaf spinach, thawed
1.5kg/3–3½lb sole or plaice to yield 675g/1½lb skinned fillets
2 white English muffins, split
60ml/4 tbsp crème fraîche
salt and ground black pepper

COOK'S TIP

Approximately half of the weight of flat fish is bone, so if buying your fish whole, ask the fishmonger to give you enough for the correct weight of boned fish.

Heat half of the butter in a saucepan, add the chopped onion and gently cook over a low heat until softened but without letting it colour at all.

Add the mushrooms and thyme, cover and cook for a further 2–3 minutes. Remove the lid and increase the heat to drive off any excess moisture. Using the back of a large spoon, press the thawed frozen spinach in a sieve to squeeze out all the liquid.

Heat a further 30ml/2 tbsp butter in a saucepan, add the spinach, heat through and season to taste.

Melt the remaining butter in a large frying pan, season the sole or plaice fillets and, with skin side uppermost, cook for 2 minutes, then turn and cook for another 2 minutes.

Toast and butter the muffins. To serve, divide the fillets among them, top with spinach and a layer of mushrooms, then finish with a generous spoonful of crème fraîche.

Fish and Shellfish

Seafood and shiitake, oyster and chestnut mushrooms make perfect partners in a fine selection of flavourful dishes, whether served as a sauce with salmon, with seafood in a savoury pilaff, or Japanese-style in tuna teriyaki.

TROUT WITH MUSHROOM SAUCE

The subtle flavour of trout is enhanced by this creamy mushroom sauce.

Serves 4

8 pink trout fillets
seasoned plain flour, for dusting
75g/3oz/6 tbsp butter
1 garlic clove, chopped
10ml/2 tsp chopped fresh sage
350g/12oz assorted mushrooms, such as button, chestnut and oyster, trimmed and sliced
90ml/6 tbsp dry white wine
250ml/8fl oz/1 cup double cream
salt and ground black pepper
sage sprigs, to garnish

COOK'S TIP

Use a large sharp knife to ease the skin from the trout fillets, then pull out any bones from the flesh – a pair of tweezers makes easy work of this fiddly task!

Remove the skin from the trout fillets, then carefully remove any bones. Lightly dust the trout fillets on both sides in the seasoned flour, shaking off any excess.

Melt the butter in a large frying pan, add the trout fillets and fry gently over a moderate heat for 4–5 minutes, turning once. Remove from the pan and keep warm. Add the chopped garlic, sage and mushrooms to the pan and gently fry until softened.

Pour in the wine and boil briskly to allow the alcohol to evaporate. Stir in the cream and season to taste with salt and pepper.

Serve the trout fillets on warmed plates with the sauce spooned over. Garnish with a few sage sprigs.

Salmon with Tarragon and Mushrooms

Tarragon has a distinctive aniseed flavour that is good with fish, cream and mushrooms. This recipe uses a selection of mushrooms to provide both texture and flavour.

Serves 4

50g/2oz/4 tbsp unsalted butter
4 × 175g/6oz salmon steaks
1 shallot, finely chopped
175g/6oz assorted mushrooms, such as oyster, shiitake, ceps and morels, trimmed and sliced
200ml/7fl oz/⅞ cup chicken or vegetable stock
10ml/2 tsp cornflour
2.5ml/½ tsp mustard
50ml/3½ tbsp crème fraîche
45ml/3 tbsp chopped fresh tarragon
5ml/1 tsp white wine vinegar
salt and cayenne pepper
new potatoes and green salad, to serve

Cook's tip

Fresh tarragon will bruise and darken after chopping, so chop just before you need it.

Melt half of the butter in a large, non-stick frying pan, season the salmon with the salt and pepper and cook over a moderate heat for 8 minutes, turning once. Transfer to a plate, cover and keep warm.

Heat the remaining butter in the pan, add the shallot and gently cook over a low heat without letting it colour. Add the mushrooms and continue to cook until the juices begin to flow. Add the chicken or vegetable stock and simmer for a further 2–3 minutes.

Put the cornflour and mustard in a cup and blend with 15ml/1 tbsp of water. Stir into the mushroom mixture and bring to a simmer, stirring continuously, to thicken. Add the crème fraîche, chopped fresh tarragon, vinegar and more seasoning.

If you like, remove the skin from the salmon steaks: insert a fork between the flesh and skin and wind the skin round the fork in a fluent action. Spoon the mushrooms over each salmon steak and serve with new potatoes and a green salad.

SEAFOOD AND MUSHROOM PILAFF

This all-in-one-pan main course is a satisfying meal for any day of the week. For a special meal, substitute dry white wine for the orange juice.

Serves 4

10ml/2 tsp olive oil
250g/9oz/generous 1 cup long grain rice
5ml/1 tsp ground turmeric
1 red pepper, seeded and diced
1 small onion, finely chopped
2 courgettes, sliced
150g/5oz button mushrooms, halved
350ml/12fl oz/$1\frac{1}{2}$ cups fish or chicken stock
150ml/$\frac{1}{4}$ pint/$\frac{2}{3}$ cup orange juice
350g/12oz white fish fillets
12 fresh mussels in the shell (or cooked, shelled mussels)
salt and ground black pepper
grated rind of 1 orange, to garnish

Heat the oil in a large, non-stick frying pan, add the rice and turmeric and sauté over a low heat for about 1 minute.

Add the pepper, onion, courgettes and mushrooms. Stir in the stock and orange juice. Bring to the boil.

Reduce the heat and add the fish. Cover and simmer gently for about 15 minutes, until the rice is tender and the liquid absorbed. Stir in the mussels and heat thoroughly. Adjust the seasoning to taste and garnish with the grated orange rind. Serve immediately.

FISH BALLS IN MUSHROOM SAUCE

This quick meal is a good choice for young children, as you can guarantee no bones.

Serves 4

450g/1lb white fish fillets, such as hoki or cod, skinned
60ml/4 tbsp fresh wholemeal breadcrumbs
30ml/2 tbsp snipped fresh chives or finely chopped spring onions
400g/14oz can chopped tomatoes
50g/2oz button mushrooms, sliced
salt and ground black pepper
snipped fresh chives, to garnish
mange-touts, to serve

COOK'S TIP

Instead of using a can of chopped tomatoes and fresh mushrooms, you could substitute a jar of ready-made tomato and mushroom sauce. Just add the fish balls and simmer gently for 10 minutes.

Cut the fish fillets into large chunks and place in a food processor. Add the wholemeal breadcrumbs and snipped chives or chopped spring onions. Season to taste with salt and black pepper, and process until the fish is finely chopped but still has some texture left.

Divide the fish mixture into about 16 even-size pieces, then mould them into balls with your hands.

Place the tomatoes and mushrooms in a wide saucepan and cook over a moderate heat until boiling. Add the fish balls, cover and simmer for about 10 minutes until cooked. Serve hot, garnished with snipped fresh chives and accompanied by mange-touts.

TUNA SHIITAKE TERIYAKI

Teriyaki is a sweet soy marinade usually used to glaze meat. Here teriyaki enhances fresh tuna steaks served with rich shiitake mushrooms.

Serves 4

4 × 175g/6oz fresh tuna or yellow tail steaks
pinch of salt
175g/6oz shiitake mushrooms, sliced
150ml/¼ pint/⅔ cup teriyaki sauce
225g/8oz white radish, peeled
2 large carrots, peeled
plain boiled rice, to serve

Place the tuna or yellow tail steaks in a shallow dish and season them with a sprinkling of salt, then set aside for about 20 minutes for the salt to penetrate. Add the sliced mushrooms to the dish and pour the teriyaki sauce over the fish steaks and mushrooms. Leave to marinate for a further 20–30 minutes or for longer if you have the time.

Preheat a moderate grill or barbecue. Remove the fish steaks from the marinade and reserve the marinade. Grill or barbecue the fish for 8 minutes, turning once.

Transfer the mushrooms and marinade to a stainless steel saucepan and simmer for about 3–4 minutes.

Slice the white radish and carrots thinly, then shred the vegetables finely with a chopping knife. Arrange a heap of each on four serving plates and add the fish steaks, with the mushrooms and sauce poured over. Serve at once with plain boiled rice.

COOK'S TIP

One of the finest teriyaki sauces is made by the company Kikkoman and can be found in most large supermarkets.

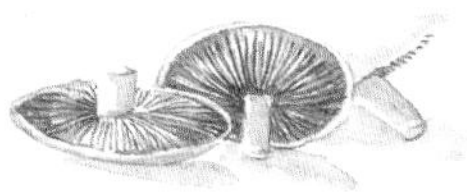

Meat and Poultry

Superbly creamy stroganoff; fricassée with rich woodland flavours; aromatic, herbed rösti; tender beef in wine with a crisp pastry topping; wild mushroom plait and a delectable filet mignon are some of the delights on offer.

BEEF AND MUSHROOM STROGANOFF

A version of the classic recipe for stroganoff, made with fillet steak, wild mushrooms and cream.

Serves 4

450g/1lb fillet steak, trimmed and cut into thin strips
30ml/2 tbsp olive oil
45ml/3 tbsp brandy
2 shallots, finely chopped
225g/8oz oyster mushrooms, trimmed and halved
150ml/¼ pint/⅔ cup beef stock
75ml/5 tbsp soured cream
5ml/1 tsp Dijon mustard
½ sweet gherkin, chopped
45ml/3 tbsp chopped fresh parsley
salt and ground black pepper
buttered noodles and poppy seeds, to serve

COOK'S TIP

If you don't want to go to the expense of buying fillet steak, choose either best rump or sirloin instead.

Season the steak with pepper. Heat half of the oil in a large, heavy-based frying pan and cook for 2 minutes. Transfer the meat to a plate.

Place the frying pan over a moderately high heat and brown the sediment. Stand back from the pan, add the brandy, tilt towards the flame (or ignite with a match if cooking on an electric hob) and burn off the alcohol vapour. Pour these juices over the meat, cover and keep warm.

Wipe the pan clean. Heat the remaining oil, add the shallots and fry until lightly brown. Add the mushrooms and cook for 3–4 minutes to soften.

Pour over the stock and simmer for a few minutes more and then add the soured cream, mustard and gherkin together with the steak and its juices. Simmer briefly, season to taste with salt and pepper and stir in the chopped parsley. Serve with buttered noodles garnished with poppy seeds.

Chicken and Mushroom Fricassee

A fricassée is a light stew, here accompanied by a sauce with a rich woodland flavour.

Serves 4

3 × 115g/4oz chicken breasts, sliced
115g/4oz unsmoked rindless streaky bacon, cut into pieces
50g/2oz/4 tbsp unsalted butter
15ml/1 tbsp vegetable oil
75ml/5 tbsp dry sherry or white wine
1 onion, chopped
350g/12oz assorted mushrooms, such as ceps, closed cup and oyster, trimmed and sliced
45ml/3 tbsp plain flour
500ml/18fl oz/2¼ cups chicken stock
10ml/2 tsp lemon juice
60ml/4 tbsp chopped fresh parsley
salt and ground black pepper
plain boiled rice, carrots and baby sweetcorn, to serve

In a flameproof casserole, brown the chicken and bacon in half of the butter and the oil. Place in a shallow dish and pour off any excess fat.

Return the casserole to the heat and brown the sediment. Pour in the sherry or wine and stir with a flat wooden spoon to deglaze the pan. Pour the liquid over the chicken and wipe the casserole clean.

Fry the onion in the remaining butter until golden brown. Add the mushrooms and cook, stirring frequently, for about 6–8 minutes or until their juices begin to run. Stir in the flour then remove the pan from the heat. Gradually add the chicken stock and stir well until the flour is absorbed.

Add the chicken and bacon with the juices, return to the heat and stir to thicken. Simmer for 10–15 minutes and then add the lemon juice, parsley and seasoning. Serve with boiled rice, carrots and baby sweetcorn.

MUSHROOM ROSTI WITH BACON

Dried ceps or porcini mushrooms, commonly found in Italian delicatessens, are a good substitute for fresh.

Serves 4

675g/1½lb floury potatoes, peeled
10g/¼oz dried ceps or porcini
2 fresh thyme sprigs, chopped
30ml/2 tbsp chopped fresh parsley
60ml/4 tbsp vegetable oil, for frying
4 × 115g/4oz unsmoked bacon rashers
pinch of salt
4 eggs, to serve
1 bunch watercress, to serve

COOK'S TIP

A large rösti can be made in a non-stick frying pan. Allow 12 minutes to cook. Halfway through the cooking time, invert the rösti on to a large plate and slide back into the pan.

Bring the potatoes to the boil in a large saucepan of salted water and cook for 5 minutes. Meanwhile, cover the mushrooms with boiling water to soften. Drain, then chop them roughly.

Drain the potatoes, allow them to cool and grate them coarsely. Add the mushrooms, thyme and parsley and mix together well.

Heat 30ml/2 tbsp of the oil in a frying pan, spoon in the rösti mixture in heaps and flatten. Fry for 6 minutes, turning once during cooking.

Preheat a moderate grill and cook the bacon rashers until sizzling. Heat the remaining oil in a frying pan and fry the eggs as you like them. Serve the rösti together with the eggs and bacon and watercress.

STEAK AND MUSHROOM PIE

Tender chunks of beef are cooked in a rich mushroom and wine sauce. The crisp filo pastry crust makes a change from the more traditional shortcrust or puff pastry topping.

Serves 4

1 onion, finely chopped
175ml/6fl oz/¾ cup beef stock
450g/1lb lean chuck steak, cut into 2.5cm/1in cubes
120ml/4fl oz/½ cup dry red wine
45ml/3 tbsp plain flour
225g/8oz button mushrooms, halved
5 sheets filo pastry
10ml/2 tsp sunflower oil
salt and ground black pepper
mashed potatoes and runner beans, to serve

Simmer the onion with 120ml/4fl oz/½ cup of the stock in a large, covered, non-stick saucepan for 5 minutes. Uncover and continue to cook, stirring occasionally, until the stock has reduced entirely. Transfer the onion to a plate and set aside until required.

Add the steak to the saucepan and dry-fry until the meat is lightly browned. Return the onion to the saucepan together with the remaining stock and the red wine. Cover and simmer gently for about 1½ hours, or until the meat is tender.

Preheat the oven to 190°C/375°F/Gas 5. Blend the flour with 45ml/3 tbsp of cold water, add to the saucepan and continue to simmer, stirring all the time, until the sauce has thickened.

Add the mushrooms and continue to cook for 3 minutes. Season to taste with salt and pepper and spoon into a 1.2 litre/2 pint/5 cup pie dish.

Brush a sheet of filo pastry with a little of the sunflower oil, then crumple it up loosely and place oil-side up over the filling. Repeat with the remaining sheets of pastry and oil.

Bake in the oven for about 25–30 minutes until the pastry is golden brown and crispy. Serve with creamy mashed potatoes and freshly cooked runner beans.

SAUSAGE AND MUSHROOM PLAIT

Fresh pork sausages needn't be cooked in their skins. To make the most of them, remove the meat and wrap it in a puff pastry parcel. A thick seam of wild mushrooms is a delicious addition.

Serves 4

50g/2oz/4 tbsp unsalted butter
½ garlic clove, crushed
15ml/1 tbsp chopped fresh thyme
450g/1lb assorted mushrooms, such as ceps, oyster and button, trimmed and sliced
50g/2oz/1 cup fresh white breadcrumbs
75ml/5 tbsp chopped fresh parsley
350g/12oz puff pastry, thawed if frozen
675g/1½lb pork sausages
1 egg, beaten with a pinch of salt
salt and ground black pepper

Preheat the oven to 180°C/350°F/Gas 4. Heat the butter in a large, non-stick frying pan, add the crushed garlic, chopped thyme and sliced mushrooms and gently cook over a low heat for 5–6 minutes until soft but not browned. When the mushroom juices begin to run, increase the heat to evaporate the juices. When quite dry, stir in the breadcrumbs and chopped parsley and season well with salt and black pepper.

Roll the pastry out on a floured surface to form a 36 × 25cm/14 × 10in rectangle and place on a large baking sheet.

Remove the skins from the sausages and discard. Place half of the sausagemeat in a 13cm/5in strip along the centre of the pastry. Cover with the mushroom mixture, then put another layer of sausagemeat over the mushrooms.

Make a series of 2.5cm/1in slanting cuts in the pastry on each side of the filling. Fold the two ends of pastry over the filling, moisten the pastry with beaten egg and then cross the top with alternate strips of pastry from each side. Allow to rest for 40 minutes, brush with a little more egg and bake in the oven for 1 hour. Serve immediately.

COOK'S TIP

A good pinch of salt added to a beaten egg will break it down and improve the finished glaze.

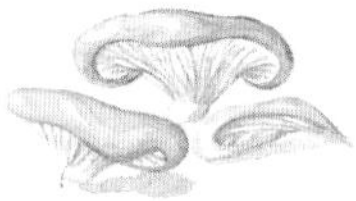

FILET MIGNON WITH MUSHROOMS

Large mushroom caps are readily available and look attractive especially when they are fluted as in this dish.

Serves 4

4 thin slices white bread
115g/4oz pâté de foie gras *or* mousse de foie gras
4 closed cup mushrooms
65g/2½oz/5 tbsp butter
10ml/2 tsp vegetable oil
4 fillet steaks (about 2.5cm/1in thick)
45–60ml/3–4 tbsp Madeira or port
120ml/4fl oz/½ cup beef stock
bunch of watercress, to garnish

Cut the bread into rounds about the same diameter as the steaks, using a large round cutter or by cutting into squares, then cutting off the corners with a sharp knife. Toast the bread and spread with the *foie gras* or *mousse de foie gras*, dividing it evenly. Place the croûtons on warmed plates.

Flute the mushrooms using a small, sharp knife, if you wish, for a decorative effect. Melt 30ml/2 tbsp of the butter in a non-stick frying pan, add the mushrooms and sauté over a moderate heat until golden. Transfer to a plate and keep warm until required.

In the same pan, melt another 30ml/2 tbsp of the butter with the oil over a moderately high heat, swirling to combine. When the butter begins to brown, add the steaks and cook for about 6–8 minutes, turning once, until cooked as preferred (medium-rare meat will still be slightly soft when pressed, medium will be springy, and well-done firm). Place the steaks on top of the croûtons and top with the mushrooms.

Add the Madeira or port to the pan and boil for 20–30 seconds. Add the stock and boil over a high heat until reduced by three-quarters, then swirl in the remaining butter. To serve, pour a little sauce over each steak, then garnish with the watercress.

COOK'S TIP
If pâté de foie gras *is difficult to find, you could substitute pork liver pâté in this recipe.*

Pasta and Rice

Mushrooms add their delicate flavour to all sorts of pasta and rice dishes. With the addition of herbs, nuts, cheese, bacon and fresh vegetables, they enhance stir-fries, risottos, pasta sauces, bakes and rice salads.

SPAGHETTI WITH MUSHROOM SAUCE

The combination of mixed mushrooms and freshly chopped sweet basil tossed with spaghetti would be complemented by a fresh tomato salad.

Serves 4

50g/2oz/4 tbsp butter
1 onion, chopped
350g/12oz spaghetti
350g/12oz assorted mushrooms, such as chestnut, flat and button, sliced
1 garlic clove, chopped
300ml/½ pint/1¼ cups soured cream
30ml/2 tbsp chopped fresh basil
60ml/4 tbsp grated Parmesan cheese
salt and ground black pepper
torn flat leaf parsley, to garnish
grated Parmesan cheese, to serve

Melt the butter in a large, non-stick frying pan, add the onion and fry over a moderate heat until softened. Meanwhile, cook the pasta following the instructions on the packet.

Stir the sliced mushrooms and chopped garlic into the onion mixture and fry for a further 10 minutes until softened.

Add the soured cream, basil, Parmesan cheese and season to taste with salt and pepper. Cover and heat through.

Drain the pasta thoroughly and toss it with the sauce. Garnish with torn flat leaf parsley. Serve immediately, with plenty of Parmesan cheese.

Pasta with Mushrooms and Chorizo

The delicious combination of mushrooms and spicy sausage makes this a tempting supper dish.

Serves 4

60ml/4 tbsp olive oil
1 garlic clove, chopped
1 celery stick, chopped
350g/12oz pasta twists
225g/8oz chorizo sausage, sliced
225g/8oz assorted mushrooms, such as oyster, chestnut and shiitake
15ml/1 tbsp lemon juice
30ml/2 tbsp chopped fresh oregano
salt and ground black pepper
finely chopped fresh parsley, to garnish

Heat the oil in a large, non-stick frying pan, add the garlic and celery and cook over a moderate heat for 5 minutes until softened. Meanwhile, cook the pasta following the instructions on the packet. When cooked, strain and keep warm until required.

Add the chorizo sausage to the garlic and celery and cook for a further 5 minutes, stirring occasionally until browned.

Add the mushrooms and cook for a further 4 minutes, stirring occasionally until slightly softened. Stir in the remaining ingredients, except the garnish, and cook until heated through.

Add the pasta twists to the pan and toss thoroughly with the mushroom and chorizo sausage mixture until well combined. Serve immediately, garnished with the finely chopped fresh parsley.

Cook's tip

This dish is delicious served with lashings of Parmesan cheese shavings. Use any combination of mushrooms you like for this flavoursome sauce.

Nutty Rice and Mushroom Stir-fry

This delicious and substantial supper dish can be eaten hot or cold accompanied by different salads.

Serves 4–6

350g/12oz long grain rice
45ml/3 tbsp sunflower oil
1 small onion, roughly chopped
225g/8oz button mushrooms, sliced
50g/2oz/½ cup hazelnuts, roughly chopped
50g/2oz/½ cup pecan nuts, roughly chopped
50g/2oz/½ cup almonds, roughly chopped
60ml/4 tbsp chopped fresh parsley
salt and ground black pepper

Rinse the rice, then cook for about 10–12 minutes in 750ml/1¼ pints/3⅔ cups water in a saucepan with a tight-fitting lid. When cooked, refresh under cold water. Heat a wok, then add half of the oil. Heat the oil, then stir-fry the rice for 2–3 minutes. Remove and set aside.

Add the remaining oil and stir-fry the onion for another 2 minutes until softened. Add the button mushrooms and stir-fry for a further 2 minutes.

Add all the nuts and stir-fry for 1 minute. Return the rice to the wok and stir-fry for about 3 minutes. Season to taste, stir in the parsley and serve.

Macaroni Cheese with Mushrooms

Macaroni cheese is an all-time classic from the mid-week menu. Here it is served in a light creamy sauce with mushrooms and topped with pine nuts.

Serves 4

450g/1lb quick-cooking elbow macaroni
45ml/3 tbsp olive oil
225g/8oz button mushrooms, sliced
2 fresh thyme sprigs
60ml/4 tbsp plain flour
1 vegetable stock cube, crumbled
600ml/1 pint/2½ cups milk
2.5ml/½ tsp celery salt
5ml/1 tsp Dijon mustard
175g/6oz/1½ cups grated Cheddar cheese
25g/1oz/¼ cup grated Parmesan cheese
25g/1oz/¼ cup pine nuts
salt and ground black pepper

Cook the macaroni following the instructions on the packet. Heat the oil in a heavy-based saucepan, add the mushrooms and thyme, cover and cook over a low heat for 2–3 minutes. Stir in the flour and remove from the heat, add the stock cube and stir continuously until evenly blended. Add the milk a little at a time, stirring after each addition. Add the celery salt, mustard and Cheddar cheese and season to taste with salt and pepper. Stir and simmer briefly for 1–2 minutes until thickened.

Preheat the grill. Drain the pasta, toss into the sauce and fill four individual dishes or one large flameproof gratin dish. Scatter over the Parmesan cheese and pine nuts; grill until brown and bubbly. Serve immediately.

Mushroom and Bacon Risotto

Mixed mushrooms and smoked bacon add savoury flavour to this classic risotto.

Serves 4

30ml/2 tbsp sunflower oil
1 large onion, chopped
75g/3oz smoked bacon, chopped
350g/12oz arborio or risotto rice
1–2 garlic cloves, crushed
15g/½oz dried sliced mushrooms, soaked in a little boiling water
175g/6oz assorted mushrooms, such as button and chestnut
1.2 litres/2 pints/5 cups hot stock
a few sprigs of oregano or thyme
15ml/1 tbsp butter
a little dry white wine
45ml/3 tbsp chopped, peeled tomato
8–10 black olives, stoned and quartered
salt and ground black pepper
thyme sprigs, to garnish

Heat the oil in a large, heavy-based pan with a lid. Gently cook the onion and bacon until the onion is tender and the bacon fat has run out.

Stir in the rice and garlic and cook over a high heat for 2–3 minutes until the rice is well coated. Add the dried mushrooms and their liquid, the fresh mushrooms and half of the stock, the oregano and seasoning. Bring gently to the boil, then reduce the heat. Cover tightly and leave to cook.

Gently stir the risotto. If quite dry, slowly add more liquid. (Don't stir too often, as this lets the steam and flavour out.) Add more liquid as required until the rice is cooked, but not mushy.

Just before serving, stir in the butter, white wine, tomato and olives and taste for seasoning. Serve hot, garnished with thyme sprigs.

MUSHROOMS WITH WILD RICE

Grilling brings out the flavour of the summer vegetables in this recipe.

Serves 4

115g/4oz/scant ½ cup wild rice
115g/4oz/scant ½ cup long grain rice
1 large aubergine, thickly sliced
1 red, 1 yellow and 1 green pepper, seeded and cut into quarters
2 red onions, sliced
225g/8oz chestnut or shiitake mushrooms
2 small courgettes, cut in half lengthways
olive oil, for brushing

For the dressing

90ml/6 tbsp extra virgin olive oil
30ml/2 tbsp balsamic vinegar
2 garlic cloves, crushed
salt and ground black pepper

Put the wild rice in a saucepan of cold salted water. Bring to the boil, then reduce the heat, cover, and cook gently for 40 minutes before adding the long grain rice. Cook for a further 10 minutes, or until the grains are tender.

For the dressing, mix all the ingredients in a screw-top jar. Then arrange the vegetables on a grill rack, brush with olive oil and grill for 8–10 minutes, until tender and well browned, turning them occasionally and brushing again with oil.

Drain the rice and toss in half of the dressing. Tip into a serving dish and arrange the grilled vegetables on top. Pour over the remaining dressing and serve immediately.

Vegetable Dishes

A variety of wild and cultivated mushrooms demonstrate their amazing versatility in a diverse array of recipes, from bean dishes to burgers, roulades to ragoûts, pizza to pies, and from strudel to sautées and soufflés.

Mixed Mushroom Ragout

These mushrooms are delicious served hot or cold and can be prepared up to two days in advance.

Serves 4

1 small onion, finely chopped
1 garlic clove, crushed
5ml/1 tsp coriander seeds, crushed
30ml/2 tbsp red wine vinegar
15ml/1 tbsp soy sauce
15ml/1 tbsp dry sherry
10ml/2 tsp tomato purée
10ml/2 tsp soft light brown sugar
150ml/¼ pint/⅔ cup vegetable stock
115g/4oz baby button mushrooms
115g/4oz chestnut mushrooms, quartered
115g/4oz oyster mushrooms, sliced
salt and ground black pepper
coriander sprig, to garnish

Put the first nine ingredients into a large, heavy-based saucepan. Bring to the boil and reduce the heat. Cover and simmer for 5 minutes.

Uncover the saucepan and simmer for a further 5 minutes, or until the liquid has reduced by half.

Add the baby button and chestnut mushrooms and simmer for 3 minutes more. Stir in the oyster mushrooms and cook for a further 2 minutes.

Remove the mushrooms with a slotted spoon and transfer them to a serving dish. Boil the juices for about 5 minutes, or until reduced to about 75ml/5 tbsp. Season to taste.

Allow the juices to cool for 2–3 minutes, then pour over the mushrooms. Serve hot or well chilled, garnished with a sprig of fresh coriander.

MUSHROOM TART

The region of Alsace in France is renowned for its abundance of wild mushrooms. This tart is good with a cool Alsatian wine. Serve with baked potatoes and a mixed salad, if you like.

Serves 4

350g/12oz shortcrust pastry, thawed if frozen
50g/2oz/4 tbsp unsalted butter
3 onions, halved and sliced
350g/12oz assorted mushrooms, such as ceps, morels, oyster and button
1 thyme sprig, chopped
pinch of grated nutmeg
50ml/3½ tbsp full-fat milk
50ml/3½ tbsp single cream
1 egg and 2 egg yolks
salt and ground black pepper

COOK'S TIP

To prepare ahead, the flan case can be part-baked and the filling made in advance.

Preheat the oven to 190°C/375°F/Gas 5 and lightly grease a 23cm/9in loose-based flan tin with butter. Roll out the pastry on a lightly floured board and line the tin. Rest the pastry in the fridge for 1 hour.

Place three squares of greaseproof paper in the flan case, fill with rice or baking beans and bake blind for 25 minutes. Lift out the paper and rice or beans and leave to cool.

Melt the butter in a large, non-stick frying pan, add the onions, cover and cook slowly for 20 minutes. Add the mushrooms and thyme, and continue cooking for a further 10 minutes. Season to taste with the salt and pepper. Add the nutmeg.

Pour the milk and cream into a jug and beat in the egg and egg yolks. Place the mushroom mixture in the flan case and then pour over the milk and egg mixture. Bake for 15–20 minutes until the centre is firm to the touch. Serve hot or leave to cool before serving.

Borlotti Beans with Mushrooms

The mixture of mushrooms in this dish helps to give it a wonderfully rich and nutty flavour.

Serves 4

30ml/2 tbsp olive oil
50g/2oz/4 tbsp butter
2 shallots, chopped
2–3 garlic cloves, crushed
675g/1½lb assorted mushrooms, such as button, chestnut and oyster, thickly sliced
4 pieces sun-dried tomatoes in oil, drained and chopped
90ml/6 tbsp dry white wine
400g/14oz can borlotti beans, drained
25ml/1½ tbsp grated Parmesan cheese
30ml/2 tbsp chopped fresh parsley
salt and ground black pepper
freshly cooked pappardelle pasta, to serve

Heat the oil and melt the butter in a large, non-stick frying pan, add the shallots and fry until softened. Add the garlic and mushrooms to the pan and fry for 3–4 minutes. Stir in the sun-dried tomatoes and wine and season to taste with salt and black pepper.

Stir in the borlotti beans and cook for a further 5–6 minutes, until most of the liquid has evaporated and the beans are warmed through.

Stir in the grated Parmesan cheese. Sprinkle with the chopped fresh parsley and serve immediately with pappardelle.

Sauteed Mushrooms

This is a quick dish to prepare and makes an ideal accompaniment to all kinds of roast and grilled meats. Use any combination of mushrooms you can find.

Serves 6

900g/2lb assorted fresh mushrooms, such as morels, ceps, oyster or shiitake
30ml/2 tbsp olive oil
25g/1oz/2 tbsp unsalted butter
2 garlic cloves, finely chopped
3–4 shallots, finely chopped
45–60ml/3–4 tbsp chopped fresh parsley, or a mixture of fresh herbs
salt and ground black pepper

Wash and carefully dry any very dirty mushrooms. Trim the stems and cut the mushrooms into quarters or slice if very large.

Heat the oil in a large, heavy-based frying pan, add the butter and swirl it to melt over a moderate heat. Stir in the assorted mushrooms and then cook for 4–5 minutes until starting to brown.

Add the garlic and shallots and cook for a further 4–5 minutes until the mushrooms are tender and any liquid given off has evaporated. Season to taste with salt and pepper and stir in the parsley or mixed herbs.

MUSHROOM AND CHEESE SOUFFLE PIE

A sophisticated mushroom flan with a cheese soufflé topping. Serve hot with a cranberry relish.

Serves 8

225g/8oz/2 cups plain flour
175g/6oz/¾ cup butter
115g/4oz/1 cup grated Parmesan cheese
1 egg
15ml/1 tbsp Dijon mustard

For the filling

25g/1oz/2 tbsp butter
1 onion, finely chopped
350g/12oz mushrooms, chopped
15ml/1 tbsp chopped fresh parsley
50g/2oz/1 cup fresh white breadcrumbs
salt and ground black pepper

For the cheese topping

25g/1oz/2 tbsp butter
30ml/2 tbsp plain flour
300ml/½ pint/1¼ cups milk
30ml/2 tbsp grated Parmesan cheese
75g/3oz/¾ cup grated Cheddar cheese
1 egg, separated

To make the pastry, sift the flour into a bowl and rub in the butter until the mixture resembles fine breadcrumbs. Stir in the Parmesan cheese. Beat the egg with 15ml/1 tbsp water. Add to the flour mixture and bind to a soft pliable dough. Knead until smooth, wrap and chill for 30 minutes.

To make the filling, melt the butter in a large, non-stick frying pan, add the onion and cook over a moderate heat until tender. Add the chopped mushrooms and cook, uncovered, for 5 minutes, stirring occasionally. Increase the heat and drive off any liquid in the pan. Remove the pan from the heat and stir in the chopped fresh parsley, breadcrumbs and seasoning. Allow to cool.

Preheat a baking sheet in the oven at 190°C/375°F/Gas 5. Lightly grease a 23cm/9in loose-based flan tin. Roll the pastry out on a lightly floured board and line the tin. Rest the pastry in the fridge for 1 hour.

To make the cheese topping, melt the butter in a saucepan, stir in the flour and cook over a low heat for 2 minutes. Gradually blend in the milk. Bring to the boil to thicken, and simmer for 2–3 minutes. Remove the pan from the heat and stir in the Parmesan and Cheddar cheeses and the egg yolk and season well. Beat until smooth. Whisk the egg white until it holds soft peaks; fold the egg white into the topping.

To assemble the pie, spread the Dijon mustard evenly over the base of the flan case. Spoon in the mushroom filling and level the surface. Pour over the cheese topping and bake the pie on the hot baking sheet for 35–45 minutes until set and golden.

Mushroom and Cheese Strudel

Based on a traditional Russian dish called Koulibiac, *this makes a perfect vegetarian main course or an unusual accompaniment to cold leftover turkey or sliced ham.*

Serves 4

175g/6oz/¾ cup long grain rice
25g/1oz/2 tbsp butter
1–2 leeks, thinly sliced
350g/12oz mushrooms, sliced
225g/8oz/2 cups grated Gruyère or Cheddar cheese
225g/8oz feta cheese, cubed
30ml/2 tbsp currants
50g/2oz/½ cup chopped almonds or hazelnuts, toasted
30ml/2 tbsp chopped fresh parsley
275g/10oz frozen filo pastry, thawed
30ml/2 tbsp olive oil
salt and ground black pepper

Cook the rice in boiling salted water for 10–12 minutes until tender. Drain, rinse under cold running water and set aside. Melt the butter in a saucepan, add the leeks and mushrooms and cook over a moderate heat for 5 minutes. Transfer to a bowl to cool.

Add the well-drained rice, the cheeses, currants, toasted nuts, and parsley, and season to taste (be careful with the salt as the feta cheese is very salty).

Preheat the oven to 190°C/375°F/Gas 5. Unwrap the filo pastry. Cover it with a piece of clear film and a damp dish towel while you work. Lay a sheet of filo pastry on a large piece of greaseproof paper and brush it with oil. Lay a second sheet on the paper, overlapping the first by 2.5cm/1in. Arrange another sheet with its long side running at right angles to the long sides of the first two. Lay a fourth sheet in the same way, overlapping by 2.5cm/1in. Continue in this way, alternating the layers of two sheets so that the join between the two sheets runs in the opposite direction for each layer.

Place the filling along the centre of the pastry and shape it neatly with your hands into a rectangle about 10 × 30cm/4 × 12in.

Fold the pastry over the filling and roll the strudel over, with the help of the greaseproof paper, so that the join is hidden underneath.

Lift the strudel on to a greased baking sheet and tuck the edges under so that the filling does not leak out during cooking. Brush with oil and bake for 30–40 minutes, until golden and crisp. Let the strudel stand for 5 minutes before cutting into generous slices.

Spinach and Mushroom Souffle

Mushrooms combine especially well with eggs and spinach in this sensational soufflé. Almost any combination of mushrooms can be used, although the firmer varieties provide the best texture.

Serves 4

225g/8oz fresh spinach, washed, or 115g/4oz frozen chopped spinach
50g/2oz/4 tbsp unsalted butter, plus extra for greasing
1 garlic clove, crushed
175g/6oz assorted mushrooms, such as ceps, oyster and button
200ml/7fl oz/scant 1 cup milk
45ml/3 tbsp plain flour
6 eggs, separated
pinch of grated nutmeg
30ml/2 tbsp grated Parmesan cheese
salt and ground black pepper

COOK'S TIP

The soufflé base can be prepared up to 12 hours in advance and reheated before the beaten egg whites are folded in.

Preheat the oven to 190°C/375°F/Gas 5. Steam the spinach over a moderate heat for 3–4 minutes. Cool under running water, then drain. Press out as much liquid as you can with the back of a large spoon and then chop finely. If using frozen spinach, defrost, then squeeze dry in the same way.

Melt the butter in a saucepan, add the garlic and mushrooms and cook over a moderate heat until softened. Turn up the heat until the juices have evaporated. When dry, add the spinach and transfer the mixture to a bowl. Cover and keep warm until required.

Measure 45ml/3 tbsp of the milk into a bowl. Bring the remainder to the boil. Stir the flour and egg yolks into the cold milk and blend well. Stir the boiling milk into the egg and flour mixture, return to the pan and simmer to thicken, stirring constantly. Add the spinach mixture. Season with salt, pepper and nutmeg.

Butter a 900ml/1½ pint/3¾ cup soufflé dish, paying particular attention to the sides. Sprinkle with a little of the Parmesan. Set aside.

Whisk the egg whites until stiff. Bring the spinach mixture back to the boil, then remove from the heat. Stir in a spoonful of beaten egg white, then fold the mixture into the remaining egg white. Turn into the soufflé dish, spread level, scatter over the remaining Parmesan and bake in the oven for about 25 minutes until well risen and golden. Serve the soufflé immediately.

MUSHROOM BURGERS

Any kind of mushroom can be used in this popular dish.

Serves 4

115g/4oz mushrooms, finely chopped
1 small onion, chopped
1 small courgette, chopped
1 carrot, chopped
25g/1oz/¼ cup unsalted peanuts or cashew nuts
115g/4oz/2 cups fresh breadcrumbs
30ml/2 tbsp chopped fresh parsley
5ml/1 tsp yeast extract
fine oatmeal or flour, for shaping
salt and ground black pepper
green salad, to serve

Cook the mushrooms in a non-stick frying pan without oil, stirring, for 8–10 minutes to remove all the moisture.

In a food processor, process the onion, courgette, carrot and nuts until beginning to bind together. Stir in the mushrooms, breadcrumbs, parsley and yeast extract and season to taste with salt and pepper. With the oatmeal or flour, shape into four burgers. Chill in the fridge.

Cook the burgers in a non-stick frying pan with very little oil or under a hot grill for 8–10 minutes, turning once, until the burgers are cooked and golden brown. Serve hot with a green salad.

COOK'S TIP

You can prepare these burgers up to a day before cooking. Arrange them on a plate or tray and cover with clear film, then chill until ready to cook.

Chicken and Shiitake Pizza

The addition of shiitake mushrooms adds an earthy flavour to this colourful pizza, while fresh red chilli makes a fiery addition, which you may wish to omit.

Serves 3–4

45ml/3 tbsp olive oil
350g/12oz chicken breast fillets, skinned and cut into thin strips
1 bunch spring onions, sliced
1 fresh red chilli, seeded and chopped
1 red pepper, seeded and cut into thin strips
75g/3oz shiitake mushrooms, wiped and sliced
45–60ml/3–4 tbsp chopped fresh coriander
1 pizza base, about 25–30cm/10–12in diameter
15ml/1 tbsp chilli oil
150g/5oz mozzarella cheese
salt and ground black pepper

Preheat the oven to 220°C/425°F/Gas 7. Heat 30ml/2 tbsp of the olive oil in a wok or large frying pan, add the chicken, spring onions, chilli, pepper and mushrooms and stir-fry over a high heat for 2–3 minutes until the chicken is firm but still slightly pink within. Season to taste with salt and pepper.

Pour off any excess oil, then set aside the chicken mixture to cool. Stir the fresh coriander into the chicken mixture. Brush the pizza base with the chilli oil. Spoon over the chicken mixture and drizzle over the remaining olive oil.

Grate the mozzarella and sprinkle it over the pizza. Bake for about 15–20 minutes until crisp and golden. Serve immediately.

Spinach and Mushroom Roulade

An attractive and impressive dish that is surprisingly simple to prepare.

Serves 6–8

450g/1lb fresh spinach
15g/½oz/1 tbsp butter
4 eggs, separated
pinch of grated nutmeg
50g/2oz/½ cup grated Cheddar cheese
salt and ground black pepper

For the filling

25g/1oz/2 tbsp butter
350g/12oz button mushrooms, chopped
30ml/2 tbsp plain flour
150ml/¼ pint/⅔ cup milk
45ml/3 tbsp double cream
30ml/2 tbsp snipped fresh chives

Preheat the oven to 190°C/375°F/Gas 5. Line a 23 × 33cm/9 × 13in Swiss roll tin with non-stick baking paper. Wash the spinach and remove the stalks, then cook the wet leaves in a covered pan without extra water until just tender. Drain the spinach well, squeeze out all the excess moisture and then chop finely.

Tip the spinach into a bowl, beat in the butter and egg yolks and season with salt, pepper and nutmeg. Whisk the egg whites until stiff and fold into the spinach mixture. Spread into the tin and sprinkle with half of the cheese. Bake for 10–12 minutes until just firm.

To make the filling, melt the butter in a saucepan, add the mushrooms, and fry over a moderate heat until softened. Stir in the flour and cook for 1 minute. Gradually add the milk, then bring to the boil, stirring until thickened. Simmer for a further 2–3 minutes. Remove from the heat and stir in the cream and chives.

Remove the cooked roulade from the oven and turn out on to a sheet of non-stick baking paper. Peel off the lining paper and spread the roulade evenly with the mushroom filling.

Roll up the roulade fairly tightly and transfer to an ovenproof dish. Sprinkle over the remaining cheese and return the roulade to the oven for about 4–5 minutes to melt the cheese. Serve at once, cut into slices.

INDEX